Weight of Water

poems by

Samantha Wallen

Finishing Line Press
Georgetown, Kentucky

Weight of Water

"The land knows you, even when you are lost."
—Robin Wall Kimmerer

For my mother, Tedra
For the Earth, and all mothers
who carry our weight...

Copyright © 2026 by Samantha Wallen
ISBN 979-8-89990-314-4 First Edition
All rights reserved under International and Pan-American Copyright Conventions. No part of this book may be reproduced in any manner whatsoever without written permission from the publisher, except in the case of brief quotations embodied in critical articles and reviews.

ACKNOWLEDGMENTS

Grateful acknowledgment is made to the editors of the following publications where these poems, some in earlier versions, first appeared:

Dark Mountain Project: Eight Fires: "a larger logic"
Marin Poetry Center Anthology 2020: "Leaving Princess Kaiulani Hotel"
Toad Hall Editions: Kerning | A Space for Words, No. 5: "Camphor Balm"
Toad Hall Editions: Kerning | A Space for Words, No. 3: "Tidal"
Toad Hall Editions: Kerning | A Space for Words, No. 3: "Consumed"

Publisher: Leah Huete de Maines
Editor: Christen Kincaid
Cover Art: Lorena's Rock by Alice Krasinski
Interior Art: Amy Lynn
Author Photo: Kat Bacchus, Kat Bacchus Photography
Cover Design: Elizabeth Maines McCleavy

Order online: www.finishinglinepress.com
also available on amazon.com

Author inquiries and mail orders:
Finishing Line Press
PO Box 1626
Georgetown, Kentucky 40324
USA

Contents

Ectopic 1

Blue Whale 3

Imprinted with Time 5

Tidal 6

State Road 37 8

The Wound 9

Camphor Balm 10

Leaving Princess Kaiulani Hotel 12

To Those Who Never Became 14

Fluvial Geomorphology 15

Cormorant 16

The Body Whole 17

Prayer for Decay 18

a larger logic 21

Stone Womb of the Mountain 23

To Become 25

Sea of Impermanence 26

Consumed 28

Coming to Terms 30

How Shall You Live Now? 31

Weight of Water 32

Ectopic

I dreamt of a pregnancy in my lung
fetus floating amniotic in the left superior lobe
little backbone curved against my trachea
a small landholder displacing the home of my breath

The aerial view of that embryonic isthmus
in the white florescent light of the x-ray film
its surrounding estuary of bronchial pathways
was so gorgeous—I thought I would die

How could something so precious
plant itself where it does not belong?

How could a single cell swarm into a continent
of dislocation?

There was talk of a forced removal I feared
would lead to generations of regret

I wanted to allow that tented seed of happiness
to keep its abnormal position and expand its dominion

I wanted to cultivate all those cotton fields of possibility
such unrepentant growth would bring

But I knew if I did
we would die—

The Amazon Rainforest has been
called the lungs of the earth

More than twenty percent has been removed

A large spine of deforestation
presses against our airway

There is nothing separate
about the dream
the air
the body
the extraction
we are bound up in

Blue Whale
after Eva Hooker

If polar waters, if memory tracks
shifting hot spots, if equatorial
water winter, if dinner-plate
size aorta, if 400 pound heart,
if buoyant, if heard miles away,
if he follows, if she chooses,
if they circle, if rolling underwater,
if a sudden flying upwards, if thrust,
if multiple folds open, if love, if sublime,
if she is a fibrous scar of ovulation, if
sperm, if placenta, if one inch growth per day,
if rostrum tip to tail notch, if twelve feet
in seven months, if no harpoon gun, if
no fishing gear entanglements, if born
tail first, if broad flat head, if calf nudges,
if a nipple protrudes, if milk,
if wean, if baleen plates, if keratin
sieve, if lunge feed, if six tons
of krill a day, if no ship strikes, if pale
underside yellow coat diatoms, if barnacles,
if throat pleats expand, if frequency, if song
louder than any other on the planet, if no
drilling, if no construction, if no human
made ocean noise, if no stress response,
if slender fluke, if columnar spray, if breath
seen thirty feet in the air—

then Antarctic blue, Chilean
blue, Northern blue, Pygmy blue—

if water—
carries our weight

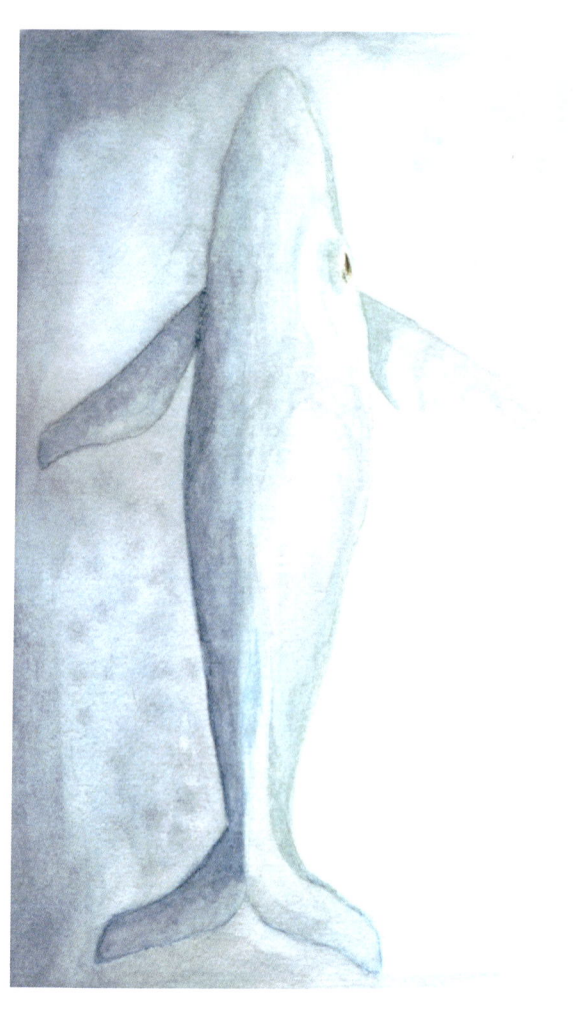

Imprinted with Time

A girl digs in the rock pile under the red mailbox
in her front yard, searching for fossil rocks inked with fern.

Hawk-like, wonder-struck, urgent, she tries
to figure out what it means to be here, imprinted with time.

She scrutinizes every rock, each one weighted
with importance. Her mother calls her, sits her down

on the brass bed with the strawberry vine comforter and says,
"I won't live past Christmas."

The girl goes to her room, climbs to the top bunk, stares
at the ceiling and imagines black holes in outer space. Her heart

pounds as she pictures herself floating toward the event
horizon, the place where lightness collapses

into darkness. "The point of no return," her third-grade teacher,
Mrs. Peters had called it. There, gravity becomes so great

escape is impossible. The girl is surprised by how good it feels
to be pressed into her bed, held down on Earth by gravity.

That pull stretches into a longing to find the lost relic
that will show her how she too might be able to unfurl fronds

complex enough to soak up light, recreate herself, keep her
dying mother alive. She piles those rocks on her dresser

and waits for their language to become hers. She picks up
a pen and begins to ink herself into a future she cannot see.

Tidal

this pattern of rising and falling
up one day, down the next as if i am tidal

yesterday welcoming the tiny red spider
skittering across the kitchen table
today wanting to kill it

yesterday's *outrush* of words
today's *inrush* of nothing to say

maybe it is the way i was named
in a story about a dying lake

maybe it is the suicide note she left
that said, "i could not solidify myself"

maybe it is how my child showed me
that out beyond male and female
there's an ocean and sometimes
taking a piece of yourself away
makes you more whole

for so many years i have sought refuge
in rock-ribbed houses childhood built

the word bay in Potawatomi language
is not a noun, not something fixed, but a verb —
wiikwegamaa is 'to *be* a bay'

maybe i *am* bay
unsolidified between shores
undulating with eelgrass, pods of pelicans
circulatory and breaking the dead shells
of yesterday

today i could become
stream, ocean, waterfall and slip through
all tidy definitions
coming to be and departing

State Road 37

A nine-mile stretch of asphalt
cuts through the north shore
of the San Pablo Bay

From Vallejo to Sears Point, rusted metal,
plastic bags, bottles and tarps strangle
the estuary's neck. So many rubber tires;
thick black scars in the mud flesh marsh

We do not have language
for the molestation of water

Two feet above tide, we drive
in cars, moving at the speed
of indecency. The salt marsh
mouse screams across the road,
understands without language
what we have done

I saw an egret
the first time I drove this road with Dad
en route from Wyoming to celebrate his 80th birthday
"I killed one of those with a slingshot," he confessed
"I regret it terribly"

What is the language
of restoration?

The tide is coming in
The animal in us knows

The Wound

i began today wondering
how to enter a wound

spoke with a woman who said
you have to look in the mirror
until you shatter

read the words of a woman who said
Earth cannot survive industrial society,
renewable energy plans are gilded green lies
still dependent upon extraction

i think of all the times a doctor said
this might pinch and feel a little cold
as the speculum slid in

it is speculated that *wound* goes way back
to an Indo-European base word
meaning *stab*

so many times i have punctured things
open, trying to flood everyplace
with a light too bright for shadow

a new moon remains hidden,
while moving oceans

perhaps we are not meant to enter,
not meant to penetrate
everything

all this pushing our way inside things
all these broken membranes

Camphor Balm

The night my husband tripped with the cast-iron pot in his hands,
spilling a cauldron of boiling water onto the top of my foot,
he left a red, open wound the size of a silver dollar. Days later,
when the burn gel had been applied, the rawness wrapped
in gauze, I picked up the new book I'd bought, *Witches, Witch-
Hunting and Women*. Eight to nine million women were burned
at the stake. Our grandmothers. Each night now my husband takes
my foot into his hands, applies a thin layer of camphor balm to the ruby
scab emerging, the way grandmothers tended injuries with herbal
medicines. "I'll never get over it," he says. Did our grandfathers inherit
a madness from watching women they love burned alive? Did they
cave beneath violence in the blood? Carry trauma to new shores?
My husband makes reparations for the burning, and I let him.
Together we accept the long occupation of healing.

Leaving Princess Kaiulani Hotel

Woke up thinking about the gold necklace
with the moon pendant I didn't buy. The music

outside still playing its invitation to come and consume
all the island has to offer. Shops on Kalakaua Ave open,

tourists fondle plastic hula girls, flowered shirts, bags and bags
of Macadamia nuts, and purchase bits of Hawaii to take home.

The *Do Not Disturb* sign hangs on the door, as it has all week.
A red-faced finch and tiny black bird squabble on the sill, a child

squeals and splashes in the pool, couple next door blares SVU
on the TV. An insatiable longing hangs over me like puffy white

clouds hang over Waikiki every morning. I stand on the lānai
looking at the whale blue sea, palm trees bent in Talasana pose,

a woman laid out on a lounge chair, pink plumerias covering her
milk-white bikini, a paperback butterflied on her chest. Suspended

seven floors above it all, I am a stranger to the island, a stranger
to others, a stranger to myself. A consumer clerks rush to meet.

We're strangers bound only by transactions—tampons, Savex,
fresh tuna poki, sparkling strawberry-lime water, tank-top, Maui

onion chips, a piece of wood carved into a rainbow. Leaving now,
I want more, to take it all with me, aware I must give up something

to get something. I didn't write the poem that woke me
the morning after I arrived and started bleeding five days early.

I let it disintegrate, its opening line, *"The island wants my blood…"*
The poem would've been my gift to Pele—*Ka wahine 'ai honua*

(earth-eating woman), my gift to the one who consumes everything
we are unable to buy or take with us. The poem would have been

a creativity of fire, an intimacy no gift shop could sell. I pack things
into my red suitcase, recall fish I saw snorkeling Hanauma Bay—

ivory brown-stripe ones, aluminum blue-yellow ones, poky purple
urchins, big-eyed coral muncher with a seaweed beard, biting

the reef loud enough for me to hear underwater. I recollect Bob
from Jacksonville giving directions, staring at my breasts, pumping

his calves up and down in the sand, a woman walking alone
on the beach, like me. I remember the couple next door, how

I'd come to know them without ever meeting. His booming laughter,
an alarm clock I came to rely on. Her moaning the day they woke me

with their lovemaking. Does this count as intimacy? Living almost
inside the room of strangers who give their pleasure away

for free? Nothing to buy or sell. Are we a community co-created
from mutual consumption, inhabiting the capital body of Honua?

Every economic transaction has two sides: each side gets something;
each side gives something up. I leave broken brass buckle sandals

in the trash, menses and a five-dollar bill on the bedsheets,
an unwritten poem. I take a suitcase of things, my longing for more.

Perhaps the song still playing as I leave Princess Kaiulani Hotel is
Aloha 'Oe—farewell to thee, sweet, gentle one living in the distance.

To Those Who Never Became

Every journey begins with the Fool—the one who walks out, arms open, head toward the sky with so much potential, right off the cliff into reality because she seeks something lacking. I once said *fighter pilot* and *corporate lawyer* when asked who I wanted to become. If you walk long enough, your clouded head clears and you meet a poet.

Fluvial Geomorphology

some people make a living
understanding how a river
shapes earth

i went to the water yesterday wanting
intimacy—to ask Coyote Creek:

who are you?

how do i say your name?

water does this beautiful thing–
waits, stills itself and reflects
everything around it

establishes mutual trust
by becoming vulnerable
to place

shapes itself with every encounter
the way liquid is not certain
the way indigenous minds
in difficult conversations
put off arriving at any conclusion
following multiple avenues of approach
until pathways no one has seen before
suddenly reveal themselves

i want to understand how
to love other human beings

the way Coyote Creek loves
Bothin Marsh all the way into
the belly of Richardson Bay

Cormorant

dives beneath the surface
finds nourishment deep
in the waters of the bay—white-capped
by brisk winds, blunt sun,
the changing tide of an economy,
one that carried us here
to a waterside table sipping
whisky, vodka tonic with lime, Shirley
Temples—foreclosed from our home,
bankrupt in our American Dream.

We watch you—
your little black body,
long crooked neck, webbed
feet, breaking the water's façade
over and over again.

With your short wings—
designed to navigate underwater,
you stay close to shore
in considerable colonies,
building home only within
these inland waters,
leaving big ocean dreams
to other birds of prey.

The Body Whole

There is a Mohave Desert in the small of your back
a Hellhole Canyon super bloom in the cavern of your skull
a Golden Gate strait between your shoulder blades
a San Andreas Fault resting between your thighs
a San Joaquin River coursing through your veins
a Mount Tamalpais rising in your spine
an Alcatraz Island floating in the center of your heart.

There is a Pacific Ocean where your face should be.

You can feel the phantom limbs of what was severed
when the first person decided to own the first piece of land
and call it his own.

I am no longer under the delusion that I can own land. I now admit
to being owned by land.

The earth will conceive us
again, and we will perceive
the body whole.

Prayer for Decay

I was the last one to inhabit the home
of my mother's body

Three days later her uterus was
surgically removed and discarded
as hazardous waste

She had become one long garland
of mensuration

Then she became too multiple
to bleed

Whose hands took
that hollow muscular organ
submerged it in chemicals
sealed it in a red plastic bag
boiled it in the autoclave and
shoved it in the incinerator?

I used to want to be
cremated

Now I want the slow decay
of burial

I want the pilfered hearts of loved ones
to take the naked carrion of my body
into their hands and wash me
in warm water with a soft cloth
wrap me in a shroud of ivory linen
place me deep in hallowed ground
and offer me back to the soil

That way the last thing I do is inhabit the home
of our mother body

I will become a sequenced strand
of sedimentation

Then I will be multiple enough to bloom
and give back some of what has been taken

a larger logic

how might we disappear, willingly
be broken eggshell
so scattered there's no way
to continue to place ourselves
at the center

how might we disappear, willingly
be crude oil bird wing
so tarred we cannot take flight
and own the sky

how might we disappear, willingly
be sea hare poisoned
so extinct there's no memory
of our clever designs
many generations from now

how might we go completely
sentient

be a larger logic
great blue heron
aplomb in the glimmer
of Pickleweed Inlet

be fine sediment
so sensitive
every depression
reshapes us

be reduced
by all this thought of saving
everything so we can be
heroes

there will be an ending
that vanishes us

i tried to disappear today,
willingly walking the shoreline
curious as sunlight how to be
heir to cloud and wind,
leave no persistent imprint

Stone Womb of the Mountain

woke up having dreamed
i was stone, so heavy
nothing could lift me

mistook it for a yearning
to be more substantial

there was a ghost
who hinge-squeaked his way
through sleep's front door
thinking he owned the place
came to my bed
climbed on top of me
shoved his face in my ear
tongued some incoherent language
and paralyzed me with density

i could not move
i could not speak
i had no voice
except the one inside my head

what if i *am* stone?

i have never had a desire
to skim the surface

i want to sink
in deep

become dense
forest thick with leaves
not ignorant
but thick as a mountain

immoveable
yet hollow enough to carry water
flow one thing into another
like adequate into aqueduct
density into destiny

To Become

when word becomes mushroom
language a tree
mind coral reef

when sentence becomes river
longing an ocean
wonder a bee

when paragraph becomes sweetgrass
opinion petals
desire wind

when story becomes ecosystem
heart an elephant
conflict eggshell

when book becomes earth
pen an eel
ego a nest

there will be a literature of restoration

Sea of Impermanence

my lips in the rearview mirror
look just like my mother's
when she headed down the highway
just to go somewhere else, rolling
the words off her tongue: *Do it Now!*

in her dying she asked me
to spend those last morning hours
toasting coconut, frothing cream
into a pie so she could taste
one last bite

i lifted the fork to her parted lips,
gave a holy mouthful to her
unholy departure

sun came in the bedroom window,
poured across the small of my back,
the day her body burned in the crematorium

outside the front door a white moth
hung on the red brick for days,
asking me to accept the strange magic
of communication between worlds

like a cormorant i turned
toward the ocean, her winds,
kept on seeking pinnacles of rock
to set my feet upon, trembling
in a commitment to live
at the watery edge
where one churning life
meets the next

Consumed

Knee deep in unread notifications,
underneath a waning pink
Scorpio moon, I scroll
upon the image
of a dead gray whale
and weep

The loss is not just her
heaving rose white mottled belly
exposed to the sky, not just
that cargo ship hull of injury
gouged in her side

She is the fifth one found dead
in the bay the last eight days
She is the only place I can look now
to see myself fully revealed
She is the only mirror
of my human condition

Her dead body honest
on the belching shore
of everlasting now is not
a selfie of peak experience
taken from a Bali island resort
or Peruvian jungle retreat, posted
in digital habit, transactional
desire to get anyone to pay
attention to an ongoing wave
of representational reality

She is not a bio hack
quick fix, singular solution
for finding a flow state,
she is my American reckoning,
the furthest back I go,

my 30 million year old
heavy water ancestor
revealing this warehouse
of nightmares I buy from

She is asking me
to uncover my role
in this history &
this present
while saying absolutely nothing
gets you off the hook

Coming to Terms

Can we come to terms
with our economics
of displacement?

Like that day
in 2009
after foreclosure
when I looked up
the root of the word *mortgage*
and discovered
it meant *death pledge*
and always had.

How Shall You Live Now?

you ask this question
on a Saturday night in quarantine
your partner in the kitchen
pouring whiskey and frying
stuffed sopapillas in hot peanut oil
dancing and singing loud and off key
to John Prine's "Illegal Smile"

you and your grown children
fold and stuff beans and cheese
into soft dough made by hand
creating with your whole bodies
a meal and a family tradition

you want to get drunk too
get loose & easy with them
but you can't because you know
your body is wounded with sensitivity
it takes you days to recover
that radiance you have always
carried with you that radiance
that knows how to live
into every answer

to maintain that radiance
is to stay sober
drink in the galaxy question
become infinitesimal
reach that deep place
that lives at the center of the pattern
see everything familiar
as if seeing for the first time
let something other
than your own mind find you
so you might become a stranger
to everything you've ever known
be surprised by every dark opening
that pulls you right back here

Weight of Water

I don't know how to say goodbye
to a glacier

how to become a traveler
of the undefiled

open mandibles
into birdsong

follow the glacier's disappearance
accompany it as it drowns

go under a continent
of white silence

I don't know how to hold the weight
of water

With Gratitude

to Finishing Line Press, for seeing the value in these poems and giving them a home

to Michelle Puckett, my fellow poet friend whose creative conversation and collaboration helped birth many of these poems

to my writing teachers and community—those who offered insights and walked alongside me in the journey of language and restoration—Sonia Sanchez, Deena Metzger, Devika Brandt, Michelle Latvala, Susie Berg, Pamela Davis, with special thanks to Reed Bye, Barb Reynolds, Nan Seymour, and Terry Lucas whose encouragement and thoughtful feedback helped bring this collection into the world

to Aaron, my number one fan and life partner who believed in me long before I did, and who gives me everything he has to give

to Haydn, who shows me what it means to fiercely care for and take a stand for all vulnerable beings, and how to be yourself without apology

to Maddie, who sees right into the heart of things, tells it like it is, brings stories alive and makes my guts ache with laughter

to Tedra, who taught me to trust my knowing, and how to hold what is too big to hold

to Bohdan, who helped me know deep in my bones what generosity feels like

to David, who shared his love of books, the virtues of a simple life, and the genes of an Olympian

to Amy Lynn, who shares my history and the soul's longing to create, and who knows what it means to stay and to live

to Debs, Mary, Gwenn, & Kristi for deep kinship and the ground of enduring friendship that makes showing up in the world with my words more meaningful and possible

to dearest Mother Earth and all her human and more than human creatures upon which this life and these words are rooted

Samantha Wallen is a poet, writer, and writing guide devoted to a literature of restoration that brings us into communion with the living world. Rooted in the essence of the Bardic tradition, she believes the role of the poet is to inspire—to help others see beyond the purely physical, to give meaning where there was none, and to awaken possibility within what seems impossible. Her work explores loss, wonder, and the sacred act of bearing witness—to a dying mother, a lost home, vanishing species, and the desecration of the earth. Through poetry, she seeks to cultivate lucid living—an awareness of the intricate web of connection between all things.

She holds an MFA from Naropa University's Jack Kerouac School of Disembodied Poetics, and her poetry has been published by *Bombay Gin, The Dark Mountain Project, Lone Mountain Literary Society,* and *Toad Hall Editions,* among others. Through writing circles, retreats, and private mentoring she guides writers worldwide to identify their voices, write books, and build sustainable and nourishing writing lives. With 30 years of mindfulness practice, Samantha nurtures writing as a personal, spiritual, and political practice.

She lives in Northern California, where she walks in the company of trees and wild creatures, and trusts in the power of words to move body and spirit into closer proximity. She seeks to share the understanding that creativity is a necessity that belongs to everyone and provides refuge and a greater sense of self and soul, especially in turbulent times. You can find her at *www.samanthawallen.com*

www.ingramcontent.com/pod-product-compliance
Lightning Source LLC
Chambersburg PA
CBRC102059150426
43195CB00007B/119